FAMOUS AMERICAN LANDMARKS

ARLINGTON NATIONAL CEMETERY

HONORING AMERICA'S HEROES

KATHRYN WALTON

PowerKiDS press
New York

Published in 2023 by The Rosen Publishing Group, Inc.
29 East 21st Street, New York, NY 10010

Portions of this work were originally authored by Jinnow Khalid and published as *Arlington National Cemetery and the Tomb of the Unknown Soldier*. All new material in this edition is authored by Kathryn Walton.

Editor: Natalie Humphrey
Designer: Michael Flynn

Photo Credits: Cover AlejandroCarnicero/Shutterstock.com; series background lukbar/Shutterstock.com; pp. 5, 13 (JFK memorial) ieronymos/Shutterstock.com; p. 7 (all) courtesy of the Library of Congress; p. 8 Andrew Prins/Shutterstock.com; p. 9 https://commons.wikimedia.org/wiki/File:William_Christman_(19569075558).jpg; p. 11 https://commons.wikimedia.org/wiki/File:Robt_E_Lee_%26_Staff_by_Brady,_1865.jpg; p. 13 (Challenger memorial) Joaquin Ossorio Castillo/Shutterstock.com; p. 14 https://en.wikipedia.org/wiki/Michael_Blassie#/media/File:USAF_First_Lieutenant_Michael_Blassie.jpg; p. 15 Kamira/Shutterstock.com; pp. 17, 19, 20 U.S. Army photo by Elizabeth Fraser/Arlington National Cemetery; p. 21 U.S. Navy photo by Petty Officer 2nd Class Huey D. Younger Jr.

Cataloging-in-Publication Data

Names: Walton, Kathryn.
Title: Arlington National Cemetery: honoring America's heroes / Kathryn Walton.
Description: New York : PowerKids Press, 2023. | Series: Famous American landmarks | Includes glossary and index.
Identifiers: ISBN 9781538387177 (pbk.) | ISBN 9781538387191 (library bound) | ISBN 9781538387184 (6pack) | ISBN 9781538387207 (ebook)
Subjects: LCSH: Arlington National Cemetery (Arlington, Va.)-Juvenile literature. | Arlington (Va.)-Buildings, structures, etc.-Juvenile literature.
Classification: LCC F234.A7 W348 2023 | DDC 975.5'295-dc23

Manufactured in the United States of America

CPSIA Compliance Information: Batch #CSPK23. For Further Information contact Rosen Publishing, New York, New York at 1-800-237-9932.

CONTENTS

IN HONOR OF THOSE LOST

Hosting the second-largest number of burials of any national cemetery, Arlington National Cemetery is one of the most famous military cemeteries in the United States. Since its founding on June 15, 1864, Arlington has become the final resting place of over 400,000 people, many of whom lost their lives fighting to protect their country.

Arlington National Cemetery serves as a place of honor and **remembrance** for all those buried there, even those who could not be identified. The Arlington House, a large **memorial** house and former **plantation**, is located on the cemetery grounds.

★ LANDMARK FACTS! ★

Arlington National Cemetery is run and administered, or managed, by the U.S. Department of the Army. The Arlington House is maintained by the National Parks Service.

ABOUT 7,000 MORE PEOPLE ARE BURIED AT ARLINGTON EACH YEAR.

IN THE BEGINNING

When plans were first made for the Arlington National Cemetery, it was meant to be a memorial and not a cemetery. Arlington House, which sits on the property, was built to honor President George Washington. The mansion, or large home, was built by his adopted grandson, George Washington Parke Custis, and was completed in 1818.

During the Civil War, around 14,000 **Union** soldiers captured the Arlington estate. At the time, Arlington House was the home of **Confederate** General Robert E. Lee. After its capture on May 24, 1861, Arlington became the Union army's military headquarters. The estate stood on Confederate soil in northern Virginia. Many Union soldiers lived in camps at the site.

OVERLOOKING THE POTOMAC RIVER AND WASHINGTON, D.C., ARLINGTON HOUSE WAS THE PERFECT SPOT FOR UNION TROOPS TO WATCH FOR CONFEDERATE TROOPS.

★ LANDMARK FACTS! ★

On the Arlington site, there was a special camp called Freedman's Village. In it, many freed slaves lived and farmed. Between 1863 and 1900, Freedman's Village changed from a **refugee** camp to a small community with schools, hospitals, churches, and social services.

FREEDMAN'S VILLAGE

THE IDEAL LOCATION

As the number of people dying from the Civil War rose, the cemeteries in Washington, D.C., were running out of space. Around the same time, Mary Anna Lee, Robert E. Lee's wife, failed to pay taxes on the Arlington estate in person. Officials put it up for sale and on January 11, 1864, the federal government bought the estate for $26,800 ($480,000 in today's currency).

SECTION 27 HOLDS SOME OF THE OLDEST GRAVES IN ARLINGTON, MANY OF WHICH ARE FROM THE CIVIL WAR.

★ LANDMARK FACTS! ★

A quartermaster is an important military job. Quartermasters are in charge of military supplies, food service, supply delivery, and a service called mortuary affairs. Mortuary affairs include identifying fallen soldiers, ensuring safe transport of these soldiers, and arranging their funerals.

Union army Quartermaster General Montgomery Meigs then picked Arlington to be the site of a new cemetery for those who died in the Civil War. On May 13, 1864, Private William Christman of the 67th Pennsylvania Infantry was the first soldier to be buried in Arlington. He died at 21 years old.

WILLIAM CHRISTMAN'S GRAVE

BUYING BACK ARLINGTON

Though Arlington was already being used as a cemetery, George Washington Custis Lee, General Lee's son, claimed the land was rightfully his. After his father's death in 1870, Custis Lee claimed the land was illegally seized from his family. He also said that, according to his grandfather's will, the land was rightfully his. The U.S. Supreme Court decided the government taking the land was illegal, and returned it to him and his family in December 1882.

But the United States government wanted Arlington to remain a cemetery. Congress bought the land back from Custis Lee on March 31, 1883, for $150,000 ($4,175,000 in today's currency). Arlington would remain the final resting place for servicemen and women and their families.

AFTER STUDYING TO BECOME A MILITARY OFFICER, GEORGE WASHINGTON CUSTIS LEE SERVED AS **AIDE-DE-CAMP** TO PRESIDENT JEFFERSON DAVIS OF THE CONFEDERACY.

A GREAT HONOR

To be buried in Arlington National Cemetery, service members must meet highly strict standards. To receive an in-ground burial in a **casket**, requirements include having died while on active duty, or having served in the military long enough to retire. Prisoners of war and those wounded in battle are also eligible, as are veterans who've received the highest military awards for valor. For some, their spouses and young children are eligible to be buried alongside them.

Some people who serve in high-level government are also eligible. The first president to be buried in Arlington was President Howard Taft. Following him, President John F. Kennedy, his wife Jacqueline Kennedy Onassis, and two of their children were also buried there.

ABOVE PRESIDENT JOHN F. KENNEDY'S GRAVE, AN ETERNAL FLAME LIT BY HIS WIFE BURNS.

★ LANDMARK FACTS! ★

A special memorial stands in Section 46 at Arlington to honor the crew of the *Challenger* space shuttle explosion. On January 28, 1986, a **mechanical** failure caused the rocket to explode during flight. All seven people on board were killed. On March 21, 1987, memorials with the astronauts' names and images were **dedicated**.

THE TOMB OF THE UNKNOWN SOLDIER

Before **DNA** testing was invented in 1984, some soldiers killed in battle couldn't be identified. In order to honor soldiers who could not be identified, the United States created a memorial for them.

In October 1921, four unknown U.S. soldiers from World War I were **exhumed** from their graves in France. A soldier who fought in World War I chose one unknown soldier from the four, all of whom were in plain caskets. On November 11, 1921, the body of the Unknown Soldier was buried in a marble tomb in Arlington.

MICHAEL JOSEPH BLASSIE

IN 1998, DNA TESTING REVEALED THE VIETNAM UNKNOWN SOLDIER WAS FIRST LIEUTENANT MICHAEL JOSEPH BLASSIE OF THE U.S. AIR FORCE.

★ LANDMARK FACTS! ★

At the Tomb of the Unknown Soldier are three crypts, or chambers that often hold bodies dedicated to World War II, the Vietnam War, and the Korean War. Beneath all three, the body of a randomly selected unknown soldier has been buried at one time.

THE TOMB GUARDS

It is an important duty to guard the Tomb of the Unknown Soldier. To become a tomb guard, a soldier must be a part of the Third U.S. Infantry Regiment, or "The Old Guard." Tomb guards must follow strict rules. They must be completely dedicated to their training program, and many soldiers who train to be a tomb guard fail.

Before they can become tomb guards, soldiers are tested on their knowledge of the job. They take exams on a ritual, or series of acts, known as the Changing of the Guard. They're also tested on uniform preparation and the history of the tomb.

THE OLD GUARD IS THE OLDEST ACTIVE-DUTY INFANTRY UNIT IN THE ARMY, SERVING THE U.S. SINCE 1784.

HERE RESTS IN

21 STEPS

When it's time for the tomb guards to change, the guards must follow a specific process. The Changing of the Guard is performed at the Tomb of the Unknown Soldier every day of the year at specific times depending on the season. First, a relief commander announces the Changing of the Guard. The commander walks up to the tomb and salutes it, then inspects the weapon of the new guard. The new guard and the old guard switch places.

The ceremony includes the new tomb guard marching 21 steps down a black mat behind the tomb. He or she then stops, turns to face east for 21 seconds, turns to face north for 21 seconds, then takes 21 steps to the other end of the mat before repeating the process.

TOMB GUARDS SERVE THE TOMB OF THE UNKNOWN SOLDIER 24 HOURS A DAY, 365 DAYS A YEAR, REGARDLESS OF THE WEATHER.

★ LANDMARK FACTS! ★

Why 21? Twenty-one symbolizes the highest military honor, the 21-gun salute. The tradition started in the 14th century as the seven-gun salute. When British military ships wanted to show they weren't hostile, they would fire all seven of their cannons until they ran out of ammunition, or firing material. On dry land, cannons at forts could fire three rounds for every one round fired from a ship. Thus, 21!

ARLINGTON NATIONAL CEMETERY TODAY

Today, Arlington National Cemetery remains a place of remembrance for those who lost their lives in service to the United States. Since its founding, it has grown to include 639 acres (258.6 ha) of land, all used to commemorate, or help people remember, the brave servicemen and women who are buried there.

EVERY YEAR, MORE THAN 3,000 MEMORIAL SERVICES AND CEREMONIES TAKE PLACE IN ARLINGTON NATIONAL CEMETERY.

In the beginning, being buried at Arlington was mainly a way to ensure service members received a proper burial even if their families couldn't afford to bring them home. In modern times, those who visit have the chance to honor lost loved ones and brave heroes who have given their lives serving their country.

GLOSSARY

aide-de-camp: A military officer who helps another high-ranking officer.

casket: A coffin, or box, in which the body of a dead person is buried.

Confederate: Having to do with the Confederate States of America during the Civil War.

dedicate To officially make a location or object a place for honoring a person or event.

DNA: A substance that carries genetic information. It's found in the cells of plants and animals.

exhumed: To remove a body from the place where it is buried.

mechanical: Having to do with machines; relating to physical movement.

memorial: A place, display, or event that serves as a way to remember someone or something that happened.

plantation: A large farm, especially in a warm area of the world.

refugee: Someone who has been forced to leave their home for reasons including religion, war, or politics.

remembrance: The act of remembering a person, thing, or event.

Union: The side of the northern states during the American Civil War.

FOR MORE INFORMATION

BOOKS

Friesen, Helen Lepp. *Veterans Day*. New York, NY: Smartbook Media Inc., 2021.

Linde, Barbara. *Arlington National Cemetery*. New York, NY: Gareth Stevens Publishing, 2019.

WEBSITES

Arlington National Cemetery
www.arlingtoncemetery.mil/#/
Learn more about Arlington National Cemetery's fascinating history.

Arlington National Cemetery Tours
www.arlingtontours.com/
Check out more facts about visiting Arlington National Cemetery, including who is buried there and how to honor them.

Publisher's note to parents and teachers: Our editors have reviewed the websites listed here to make sure they're suitable for students. However, websites may change frequently. Please note that students should always be supervised when they access the internet.

INDEX